From Burnout to

Breakthrough!

Strategies for Recovering and Rejuvenating in

High-Stress Jobs

H Mahon

Chapter Summary

Introduction

- The epidemic of burnout in high-demand jobs
- The importance of taking action before burnout becomes unmanageable
- The challenges of recovering from burnout while continuing to work in a high-stress job

Chapter 1: Understanding Burnout

- What burnout is and what causes it
- The physical, emotional, and psychological effects of burnout
- Why burnout is so prevalent in high-demand jobs

Chapter 2: Signs and Symptoms of Burnout

- How to recognize when you're experiencing burnout
- The different stages of burnout and what they look like
- The warning signs to watch out for in yourself and others

Chapter 3: The Consequences of Ignoring Burnout

- The long-term effects of burnout on your health, career, and personal life
- The risks of not addressing burnout and continuing to push yourself
- The importance of taking action before burnout becomes unmanageable

Chapter 4: Strategies for Preventing Burnout

- How to identify and prioritize your core values
- Setting healthy boundaries and saying no when necessary
- Techniques for managing stress and avoiding burnout

Chapter 5: Strategies for Recovering from Burnout

- How to assess the extent of your burnout and create a recovery plan
- Strategies for reducing stress and managing symptoms of burnout
- How to reintegrate back into work after a burnout period

Chapter 6: Creating a Sustainable Work-Life Balance

- The importance of creating a healthy work-life balance
- Techniques for managing time effectively and staying organized
- Strategies for setting goals and managing expectations

Chapter 7: Cultivating Resilience

- The importance of resilience in high-stress jobs
- Techniques for building resilience and bouncing back from setbacks
- How to stay motivated and focused during difficult times

Chapter 8: Finding Joy and Purpose in Your Work

- How to find fulfillment and meaning in your work
- Techniques for aligning your work with your core values and purpose
- The benefits of finding joy in your work for your well-being and performance

Introduction

When I first started working in Corporate America over 20 years ago, I was ambitious, driven, and eager to climb the ranks. I loved the fast-paced environment and the challenges that came with my executive level job. But as the years went by, I found myself struggling to balance the demands of work and family life. With three elementary school age kids and a marriage that was fragile at best, I was constantly juggling multiple responsibilities and battling stress on all fronts.

Then the pandemic hit, and everything changed. Like so many other workers, I was suddenly thrust into a hybrid work environment, navigating the complexities of working from home while still trying to stay connected with my team and meet all job responsibilities. The added stress of the pandemic only compounded the existing challenges, and it wasn't long before I found myself on the brink of burnout.

As someone who has experienced burnout firsthand, I know just how devastating it can be. Burnout can leave you feeling exhausted, overwhelmed, and disconnected from the people and things you once cared about. It can impact your health, your relationships, and your overall quality of life. And yet, despite the growing awareness of burnout in high-demand jobs, many workers still struggle to recognize the signs or take action before it's too late.

That's why I am writing this book. I want to help other high-stress job workers like myself avoid the pitfalls of burnout, and recover from it when it does happen. In this book, you'll find strategies for preventing burnout, recovering from burnout, and creating a sustainable work-life balance that allows you to thrive both personally and professionally.

But before we dive into those strategies, it's important to understand the scope of the burnout epidemic in high-demand jobs, the importance of taking action before burnout becomes unmanageable, and the unique challenges of recovering from burnout while continuing to work in a high-stress job. So let's explore these topics in more detail.

Chapter 1: Understanding Burnout

As someone who has experienced burnout firsthand, I know just how debilitating it can be. Burnout is a state of emotional, physical, and mental exhaustion caused by prolonged or excessive stress. It can impact every aspect of your life, from your relationships to your job performance to your overall health and well-being. But what exactly causes burnout, and why is it so prevalent in high-demand jobs?

Burnout is a complex phenomenon that can manifest differently in different people. Some of the most common symptoms of burnout include chronic fatigue, insomnia, irritability, anxiety, and depression. It's important to note, however, that burnout is not the same as depression, although the two conditions can overlap.

There are many factors that can contribute to burnout, including:

- High workload: When you're constantly working long hours, juggling multiple projects, and dealing with tight deadlines, it's easy to become overwhelmed and exhausted.
- Lack of control: If you feel like you have little control over your work environment or the tasks you're assigned, it can be challenging to stay motivated and engaged.
- Poor job fit: If your job doesn't align with your values, interests, or strengths, it can be difficult to find meaning and purpose in your work.
- Lack of support: If you feel isolated or unsupported by your colleagues or superiors, it can be tough to manage stress and stay motivated.
- Unfair treatment: If you feel like you're not being treated fairly, whether it's due to discrimination, harassment, or other forms of mistreatment, it can be challenging to maintain a positive attitude and outlook.

- Personal life stressors: If you're dealing with personal issues such as financial stress, relationship problems, or health concerns, it can exacerbate burnout symptoms.

Burnout can have significant physical health impacts. Chronic stress can increase the risk of heart disease, high blood pressure, and other cardiovascular problems. It can also compromise the immune system, making individuals more susceptible to illness and infection. Digestive issues such as acid reflux, irritable bowel syndrome, and stomach ulcers are also common among those experiencing burnout.

Burnout doesn't just impact physical health - it can also take a significant toll on one's emotional and psychological well-being. Some of the most common psychological effects of burnout include depression, which can contribute to feelings of sadness, hopelessness, and despair. Anxiety is another common effect, leading to feelings of worry, panic, and fear. Burnout can also cause irritability, frustration, and anger, and can leave individuals feeling emotionally drained and detached. It's important to address these physical, emotional and psychological effects of burnout in order to prevent further negative impacts on overall well-being.

Burnout is especially prevalent in high-demand jobs for a number of reasons. High-demand jobs often come with high levels of responsibility, pressure, and accountability. When you're constantly working to meet tight deadlines, manage complex projects, and maintain a high level of performance, it can be easy to become overwhelmed and exhausted.

High-demand jobs often require a high degree of emotional labor. Whether you're dealing with demanding clients, managing difficult colleagues, or navigating complex office politics, high-demand jobs can be emotionally draining. Finally, high-demand jobs often come with a culture of overwork and burnout. Many high-stress jobs reward employees for working long hours, sacrificing personal time, and putting work above all else. This can create a culture in which burnout is normalized and even expected.

Burnout is not just feeling tired or stressed out from work. It is a state of physical, emotional, and psychological exhaustion that can leave you feeling completely drained, both mentally and physically. Burnout is often the result of chronic stress and is characterized by feelings of cynicism, detachment, and a sense of being overwhelmed.

The physical effects of burnout can be severe, including fatigue, insomnia, headaches, and a weakened immune system. The emotional effects can be equally as damaging, leading to feelings of anxiety, depression, and a sense of hopelessness. The psychological effects of burnout can be just as devastating, with decreased job satisfaction, a lack of motivation, and a reduced sense of accomplishment.

It's no surprise that burnout is so prevalent in high-demand jobs. The pressure to perform at a high level, coupled with long hours and limited time for self-care, can quickly lead to burnout. In addition, the competitive nature of many high-demand jobs can create a work environment that is stressful and highly demanding.

In my own experience, I have felt the effects of burnout firsthand. Working long hours, trying to balance a demanding job with the needs of my family, and feeling a constant pressure to perform at a high level eventually took its toll. I found myself feeling exhausted all the time, unable to focus or be productive at work, and disconnected from the things I used to enjoy.

But the good news is that burnout is not inevitable, and there are steps you can take to prevent it or recover from it. In the following chapters, we will explore a variety of strategies that can help you recover from burnout and rejuvenate your mind and body, even while working in a high-demand job.

Chapter 2: Signs and Symptoms of Burnout

Burnout can sneak up on you, and it's not always easy to recognize the signs and symptoms when you're in the thick of it. In this chapter, we'll explore how to recognize burnout, the different stages of burnout, and the warning signs to watch out for in yourself and others.

When you're experiencing burnout, it can feel like you're just going through the motions. You may feel tired, unproductive, and unmotivated. You might find that you're more irritable than usual, or that you're struggling to concentrate. It's important to recognize these signs and take action before burnout becomes unmanageable.

One way to recognize burnout is to pay attention to your physical and emotional state. Are you feeling more tired than usual, even after a full night's sleep? Are you having trouble falling or staying asleep? Do you feel anxious or irritable for no apparent reason? Are you struggling to concentrate or remember things?

Another way to recognize burnout is to pay attention to your work habits. Are you procrastinating more than usual, or having trouble starting tasks? Are you making more mistakes than usual, or struggling to meet deadlines? Are you having trouble staying organized or managing your time effectively?

Burnout doesn't happen overnight - it's a gradual process that can take months or even years to develop. There are three stages of burnout: the honeymoon phase, the onset of stress, and chronic burnout.

During the honeymoon phase, you may feel excited and energized by your work. You might be putting in long hours and pushing yourself hard, but you're still enjoying what you're doing. However, this can quickly lead to the onset of stress, where you start to feel overwhelmed and anxious. You may begin to have trouble sleeping, and you might find yourself using unhealthy coping mechanisms such as alcohol or drugs to manage your stress.

If you don't take action during the onset of stress, you may progress to chronic burnout. At this stage, you may feel emotionally and physically exhausted, cynical, and detached. You might start to withdraw from your friends and family, and you might feel like your work doesn't matter anymore.

If you're experiencing burnout, it's important to take action before it becomes unmanageable. Here are some warning signs to watch out for:

- Physical symptoms such as headaches, stomachaches, or muscle tension
- Emotional symptoms such as irritability, anxiety, or depression
- Decreased performance or productivity at work
- Disengagement from work or social activities
- Increased use of alcohol, drugs, or food to cope with stress
- Insomnia or other sleep disturbances
- Feeling like you have no control over your work or personal life
- Feeling like you're not making a difference or that your work doesn't matter

Each woman over 40 should also be aware that burnout and perimenopause can have similar symptoms, which can make it difficult to distinguish between the two.

Common symptoms of burnout include physical and emotional exhaustion, cynicism and detachment, feelings of ineffectiveness or lack of accomplishment, and reduced productivity.

Similarly, common symptoms of perimenopause can include physical symptoms such as hot flashes, night sweats, sleep disturbances, and fatigue, as well as emotional symptoms such as irritability, anxiety, and depression. However, it's important to note that perimenopause is a biological process that affects women as they approach menopause, while burnout is a result of chronic workplace stress. If you are experiencing any of these symptoms, it's important to speak with a healthcare professional to determine the underlying cause and receive appropriate treatment.

I thought I had it all figured out - a successful career and three beautiful children. But as the years went on, the demands of my high-stress job started to take a toll on me. I was putting in long hours at the office, and when I got home, I was still tethered to my phone and laptop. I felt like I was never truly able to disconnect.

At first, I thought I was just tired. But as time went on, I started to notice other symptoms. I was irritable and short-tempered with my family, and I found myself snapping at my coworkers for no reason. I was having trouble sleeping, and I was relying more and more on caffeine to get through the day. I started to feel a sense of dread every Sunday evening, knowing that the workweek was about to start again. I began to lose interest in activities that I used to enjoy and started to withdraw from social events. I was experiencing a sense of helplessness and hopelessness, feeling like I couldn't keep up with the demands of my job and my life. It was then that I realized I was experiencing burnout.

I remember being in a meeting with my boss, trying to stay focused on the discussion at hand. But my mind was wandering, and I was having trouble keeping up with the conversation. Suddenly, I felt a wave of exhaustion wash over me, and I couldn't fight back tears that started welling up in my eyes. I quickly excused myself and went to the bathroom, where I broke down in tears. I felt completely overwhelmed and like I couldn't keep up with the demands of my job and my personal life anymore.

That moment was a wake-up call for me. I realized that I had been pushing myself too hard for too long and that I needed to make some changes to avoid burning out completely. It wasn't easy, but with a more balanced approach to my work and personal life, I was able to recover from burnout and find a healthier way of living and working.

If you're reading this book, chances are you've experienced something similar. Maybe you're feeling exhausted and overwhelmed, like you're on the brink of burning out. Or maybe you've already reached that point and are struggling to cope with the physical, emotional, and psychological effects of burnout.

Either way, it's important to recognize the signs and symptoms of burnout so you can take action before it becomes unmanageable. Burnout doesn't happen overnight, and there are typically warning signs that appear before it reaches a critical stage.

Chapter 3: The Consequences of Ignoring Burnout

At first, burnout might seem like just a temporary state of exhaustion. However, if left unchecked, it can lead to serious consequences for your health, career, and personal life. Ignoring burnout can have long-term effects that can take years to overcome.

I have experienced the consequences of ignoring burnout firsthand earlier in my career. I was working as a project manager for a large company. I was passionate about my job and was determined to prove myself as a valuable member of the team. However, as time went on, the demands of my job became overwhelming. I was constantly working long hours, taking on more responsibilities than I could handle, and sacrificing my personal time to meet deadlines. I knew I was burning out, but I didn't want to admit it to myself. I thought if I just pushed through it, things would get better. However, that was not the case.

As time went on, I started to notice the effects of burnout on my health. I was constantly fatigued, irritable, and unable to concentrate. I had trouble sleeping at night and would often wake up feeling exhausted. I started to develop physical symptoms like headaches and stomach aches. I knew that something was wrong, but I didn't want to take time off work to address it. I was afraid that if I did, I would be seen as weak and unable to handle the demands of my job.

Unfortunately, I was wrong. Ignoring my burnout only made things worse. I began to make mistakes at work and missed important deadlines. My boss started to notice and became increasingly critical of my work. My colleagues started to avoid me, and I became isolated and lonely. I was so focused on my job that I didn't realize how much my personal life was suffering. My marriage was falling apart, and my relationships with my children were strained. It wasn't until I hit rock bottom that I realized the consequences of ignoring burnout.

Ignoring burnout can have serious consequences for your health, career, and personal life. Here are some of the most common long-term effects of burnout:

Physical health: Burnout can take a toll on your physical health. Chronic stress can lead to high blood pressure, heart disease, and other cardiovascular problems. It can also compromise your immune system, making you more susceptible to illness and infection. Burnout can also lead to digestive issues such as acid reflux, irritable bowel syndrome, and stomach ulcers.

Mental health: Burnout can also have a significant impact on your mental health. It can contribute to feelings of sadness, hopelessness, and despair. It can lead to feelings of worry, panic, and fear. Burnout can cause irritability, frustration, and anger. It can leave you feeling emotionally drained and detached. In severe cases, burnout can even lead to depression and anxiety disorders.

Career: Ignoring burnout can also have negative effects on your career. Burnout can lead to poor job performance, decreased productivity, and missed deadlines. It can also lead to conflicts with coworkers and supervisors. If left unaddressed, burnout can even lead to job loss or career changes.

Personal life: Burnout can also affect your personal life. It can lead to strained relationships with family and friends. It can also lead to a lack of interest in hobbies and activities that used to bring you joy. Burnout can cause a sense of detachment and disengagement from the world around you.

Despite these risks, many people continue to push themselves and ignore the warning signs of burnout. This can be especially true in high-demand jobs, where there may be pressure to work long hours and meet tight deadlines. However, ignoring burnout can be a dangerous game to play.

If left unaddressed, burnout can spiral out of control, making it increasingly difficult to recover. Eventually, it can become unmanageable and force you to take time off from work or even leave your job entirely. By taking action early on, you can avoid these more drastic measures and recover from burnout before it becomes too severe.

Chapter 4: Strategies for Preventing Burnout

Burnout can be difficult to recover from, but it's even better to prevent it in the first place. In this chapter, we'll explore some strategies for preventing burnout before it takes hold. These strategies include identifying your core values, setting healthy boundaries, and managing stress effectively.

One of the most important steps you can take to prevent burnout is to identify your core values. Your core values are the principles and beliefs that are most important to you. When you're clear on what matters most to you, you can make better decisions about how to spend your time and energy. This clarity helps you focus on the things that matter and avoid the things that don't.

To identify your core values, ask yourself what's most important to you in life. Some common core values include family, health, career, spirituality, and personal growth. You may have other values that are important to you as well. Write down your core values and keep them in a place where you can see them regularly. Understanding your core values is essential for preventing burnout. This will help you stay focused on what matters most to you and it forms the foundation of your decision-making process and guides your actions and behaviors.

For example, you might identify your family as your top core value, followed by sustainability and doing well for people and the environment. This means that you prioritize spending time with your loved ones, and also consider the impact of your actions on the planet and those around you.

When you identify your core values, you can align your work and personal life with them. This can help you feel more fulfilled, motivated, and energized. It also helps you make decisions that are in line with your values, reducing the chances of feeling overwhelmed and burned out.

To identify your core values, begin by taking time to reflect on what truly matters to you. Ask yourself what brings you the most joy and satisfaction in life, and what motivates you to get out of bed in the morning. It's also important to consider what your non-negotiables are, or the things you simply cannot compromise on in life. However, when reflecting on these values, try to make them as specific as possible.

For example, if family is a core value for you, ask yourself what that specifically means to you. Does it mean spending quality time with your loved ones, prioritizing your children's education and personal growth, or creating a nurturing and supportive home environment? Being specific about your values can help you to better understand what you truly want to prioritize in life and help guide your decisions and actions. It's important to note that everyone's core values will look different, and that's okay. What matters most is identifying the values that align with your authentic self and bring meaning and purpose to your life.

Take some time to brainstorm and write down your core values. Once you have identified them, consider how you can incorporate them into your work and personal life. This might involve setting boundaries, saying no to commitments that don't align with your values, and prioritizing activities that are in line with what is most important to you.

Another important strategy for preventing burnout is setting healthy boundaries. This means knowing when to say no and how to protect your time and energy. When you set healthy boundaries, you're taking control of your life and prioritizing your needs.

To set healthy boundaries, start by identifying the things that drain your energy or cause you stress. This could be certain tasks or activities, certain people, or certain situations. Once you've identified these things, make a plan for how to manage them. This might mean delegating tasks, saying no to certain requests, or avoiding certain people or situations.

Working in Corporate America can be demanding and intense, often requiring long hours, constant communication, and a never-ending workload. In such an environment, it can be challenging to set healthy boundaries and maintain a work-life balance. Here are some reasons why setting boundaries can be difficult and some practical tips for overcoming those challenges.

Fear of Consequences: One reason it can be challenging to set boundaries is the fear of consequences. Many employees fear that setting boundaries could lead to negative consequences, such as being seen as uncommitted or not being considered for promotions.

Pressure to Perform: High-stress jobs often come with a high-pressure environment that can make it difficult to prioritize your well-being. When employees feel the pressure to perform, they may sacrifice their personal life and well-being, leading to burnout.

Culture of Overworking: Many companies have a culture of overworking, where employees are expected to work long hours and respond to work emails or messages outside of normal work hours. In such a culture, setting boundaries can be challenging.

Setting healthy boundaries in Corporate America can be challenging, as the culture often emphasizes working long hours and being available at all times. However, there are still ways to set boundaries and prioritize self-care in this environment.

One approach is to be strategic about when and how you communicate your boundaries. For example, instead of explicitly saying you are not available, you could schedule important personal appointments during work hours and simply say you have a prior engagement. You could also set specific times when you are available for work-related tasks, and make it clear that outside of those times, you will not be checking email or taking calls as you have other commitments. My team knows that I will leave the office at around 4.30PM every day, then I'm unavailable until 8.30PM after which I log on again for a few hours to go through emails. While I am setting clear boundaries with my availability, I am also mindful of the expectations of the high-demand culture in Corporate America. By scheduling specific times for work-related tasks and communicating my availability to my team, I am able to prioritize self-care while still being responsive to the demands of my job.

Another tactic is to practice self-care during work hours. Taking short breaks throughout the day to stretch, meditate, or go for a walk can help you recharge and reduce stress, without taking away from your productivity. Additionally, try to prioritize tasks based on their importance and urgency, so that you can focus on the most important work and let go of less important tasks that can wait.

If you are in a leadership position, you can also model healthy boundaries for your team by prioritizing work-life balance and encouraging others to do the same. This can help shift the culture within your organization and make it more acceptable to prioritize self-care which will support retention of key employees.

Overall, while it can be challenging to set healthy boundaries in Corporate America, it is possible to prioritize self-care and avoid burnout with some creativity and strategic thinking.

It is essential to be firm but polite when setting boundaries. Be clear about your needs while remaining respectful of others' needs and expectations. It is imperative to start by identifying your most important tasks and focusing on those first. Set aside specific times during the day for tasks that require your undivided attention and prioritize those over less urgent matters. Taking care of yourself is also essential to prevent burnout and maintain a healthy work-life balance. This can include getting enough sleep, eating a healthy diet, and engaging in regular physical exercise. Having a support system can help you maintain your boundaries and prevent burnout. This can include colleagues, friends, or family members who understand the demands of your job and can provide emotional support and encouragement.

Setting healthy boundaries in high-stress jobs can be challenging, but it is essential for maintaining a healthy work-life balance and preventing burnout. By prioritizing your time, communicating your boundaries, being firm but polite, practicing self-care, and creating a support system, you can successfully set and maintain healthy boundaries in Corporate America.

Finally, managing stress effectively is key to preventing burnout. There are many techniques you can use to manage stress, including exercise, meditation, deep breathing, and relaxation techniques. It's important to find what works best for you and make it a regular part of your routine.

One technique that has been shown to be particularly effective for managing stress is mindfulness meditation. This involves focusing your attention on the present moment and letting go of distracting thoughts. Regular mindfulness meditation has been shown to reduce stress and improve overall well-being.

I learned the importance of setting healthy boundaries the hard way. I used to say yes to everything, even if it meant sacrificing my own needs and priorities. I thought that being a team player meant always putting others first, but I quickly learned that this was a recipe for burnout. After several months of working long hours and constantly saying yes to requests from my boss and coworkers, I hit a wall. I was exhausted, irritable, and constantly stressed. I realized that I needed to make a change if I was going to avoid burnout.

I started by identifying my core values and making them a priority. I realized that my health, family, and personal growth were more important to me than constantly pleasing others. I also started setting boundaries by kindly saying no to requests that didn't align with my priorities. This wasn't easy at first, but I soon realized that it was necessary if I wanted to maintain my well-being.

Finally, I started using mindfulness meditation as a way to manage my stress. I found that this technique helped me stay focused and calm, even in high-pressure situations. By focusing on the present moment, I was able to let go of distracting thoughts and stay centered. Here are a few examples of mindfulness meditation exercises that you can try:

Mindful breathing: Find a quiet place where you can sit comfortably for a few minutes. Close your eyes and focus on your breath. Notice the sensation of the air moving in and out of your nostrils or the rise and fall of your chest. Whenever your mind wanders, gently bring your attention back to your breath.

Body scan: Lie down on a yoga mat or comfortable surface. Close your eyes and bring your attention to the sensations in your body. Start at the top of your head and work your way down, noticing any areas of tension or discomfort. As you become aware of each area, breathe into it and try to release any tension.

Walking meditation: Find a quiet outdoor space where you can walk undisturbed for a few minutes. Walk slowly and pay attention to the physical sensations of walking, such as the feeling of your feet against the ground or the movement of your arms. If your mind starts to wander, gently bring your attention back to the physical sensations of walking.

Mindful eating: Choose a small piece of food, such as a raisin or piece of chocolate. Hold it in your hand and examine it closely, noticing its texture, shape, and color. Then, slowly put it in your mouth and let it sit on your tongue without chewing for a few moments. As you begin to chew, pay attention to the flavors and sensations in your mouth.

Loving-kindness meditation: Sit comfortably with your eyes closed and repeat the following phrases silently to yourself: "May I be happy, may I be healthy, may I be safe, may I live with ease." After a few minutes, visualize someone you care about and repeat the phrases for them. Finally, extend the phrases to all living beings.

Physical activity is also a great way to reduce stress. Exercise releases endorphins, which can help to improve your mood and reduce feelings of stress and anxiety. Practicing yoga can help to reduce stress and improve your overall well-being. Yoga combines physical postures with deep breathing and meditation.

Effective time management can also help to reduce stress by allowing you to prioritize your tasks and reduce feelings of overwhelm. Talking to friends or family members about your stressors can help to reduce feelings of stress and provide emotional support. You can also try creative outlets - engaging in creative activities such as painting, writing, or playing music can help to reduce stress and promote feelings of well-being.

These are just a few examples of techniques for managing stress. It's important to find what works best for you and to make stress management a regular part of your routine.

Chapter 5: Strategies for Recovering from Burnout

Burnout is a significant issue in the workplace and can lead to a variety of negative consequences for individuals and organizations. Burnout is a state of physical, emotional, and mental exhaustion caused by prolonged exposure to stressful situations. It can cause a variety of symptoms, including anxiety, depression, and physical illness. If left untreated, burnout can lead to significant mental and physical health problems and can severely impact an individual's ability to perform their job.

Fortunately, recovery from burnout is possible, and there are many strategies that individuals can use to manage and recover from burnout. The first step in recovering from burnout is to assess the extent of your burnout. This assessment will help you understand the severity of your burnout and develop a plan for recovery.

One way to assess burnout is to use a burnout inventory. Burnout inventories are self-report questionnaires that measure the severity of burnout symptoms. The Maslach Burnout Inventory is a widely used burnout inventory that assesses three dimensions of burnout: emotional exhaustion, depersonalization, and reduced personal accomplishment. Emotional exhaustion refers to feelings of emotional and physical exhaustion. Depersonalization refers to feelings of detachment from work and colleagues. Reduced personal accomplishment refers to a decreased sense of competence and achievement in work.

The Maslach Burnout Inventory (MBI) is a copyrighted assessment tool, and as such, it is not typically available for free. It is important to note that administering and interpreting the MBI requires specialized training and expertise in burnout and mental health.

Another way to assess burnout is to use a self-assessment questionnaire. These questionnaires are designed to help individuals identify the symptoms of burnout and assess the severity of those symptoms. Some examples of self-assessment questionnaires include the Copenhagen Burnout Inventory and the Shirom-Melamed Burnout Measure.

Here is an example of self-assessment burnout questionnaire - read each statement and rate how often you feel this way, using the following scale:

0 = Never

1 = Rarely (once or twice a year)

2 = Sometimes (once or twice a month)

3 = Often (once or twice a week)

4 = Always (daily)

1. I feel physically and emotionally exhausted.
2. I feel like I'm not making a difference in my work or life.
3. I have trouble sleeping or have sleep disturbances.
4. I feel irritable or impatient with my colleagues, friends or family.
5. I feel unappreciated or undervalued in my job.
6. I find it difficult to concentrate or stay focused on tasks.
7. I feel emotionally detached or numb.
8. I feel cynical or critical about my work or life.
9. I have lost interest or motivation in my job or life.
10. I feel physically ill, such as experiencing headaches or stomach issues.

Scoring:

- Add up your scores for each statement to get a total score.

- If your total score is between 0-10, it suggests that you are not experiencing burnout.
- If your total score is between 11-20, it suggests that you are experiencing mild burnout.
- If your total score is between 21-30, it suggests that you are experiencing moderate burnout.
- If your total score is 31 or higher, it suggests that you are experiencing severe burnout.

Note: This self-assessment questionnaire is not a substitute for a professional diagnosis, but it can provide a helpful starting point for understanding your burnout levels. If you are concerned about your burnout levels, please consult with a healthcare professional.

Once you have assessed the extent of your burnout, you can begin to create a plan for recovery. Creating a recovery plan is an essential step in recovering from burnout. A recovery plan will help you identify the steps you need to take to manage your symptoms, reduce stress, and reintegrate back into work after a burnout period.

Identify the causes of burnout: The first step in creating a recovery plan is to identify the causes of burnout. This will help you understand what factors contribute to your burnout and develop strategies to manage those factors. Some common causes of burnout include workload, lack of control, lack of social support, and poor work-life balance.

Set realistic goals: Setting realistic goals is essential for recovering from burnout. Setting unrealistic goals can lead to frustration and exacerbate burnout symptoms. Set small, achievable goals that will help you regain a sense of control and accomplishment.

Practice self-care: Self-care is an essential part of recovering from burnout. This can include getting enough sleep, eating a healthy diet, engaging in regular physical activity, and taking time to relax and unwind.

Seek support: Seeking support from friends, family, and colleagues can help you manage symptoms of burnout and regain a sense of social support. Consider reaching out to a mental health professional for additional support.

Reducing stress is a crucial component of recovering from burnout since stress is a significant contributor to burnout. Several strategies can be adopted to alleviate stress. The first strategy is practicing relaxation techniques such as deep breathing, yoga, and meditation, which help to reduce stress levels and promote relaxation. Another strategy is taking breaks throughout the day, which can help reduce stress and boost productivity. It's crucial to take short breaks to stretch, take a walk and get some fresh air, or engage in a quick relaxation exercise like deep breathing or progressive muscle relaxation.

Taking time off work can allow for rejuvenation, and even a few minutes of relaxation can make one feel more focused and energized when back to work. One can set reminders or alarms on their phone or computer to ensure they take breaks regularly throughout the day. It's also recommended to schedule more extended breaks, such as a lunch break, into the daily routine to give oneself ample time to disconnect from work and recharge.

Seeking support from others is also essential when recovering from burnout. Since burnout can be isolating, it's crucial to seek support from friends, family, colleagues, or even a therapist. Having someone to talk to can help one feel less alone and provide them with the tools and resources to recover. Practicing self-care is also a critical aspect of recovering from burnout. This includes things like getting enough sleep, eating a healthy diet, engaging in regular exercise, and taking time for hobbies and activities that bring joy. Practicing mindfulness meditation or other relaxation techniques can also help manage stress and reduce symptoms of burnout.

Setting boundaries is another vital strategy for preventing burnout from happening again in the future. This involves setting limits on one's workload, saying no to tasks that are not essential, and taking breaks when needed. It's crucial to be clear about boundaries with colleagues and supervisors and stick to them. Lastly, it's recommended to reevaluate one's goals and priorities since burnout can be a sign that one needs to make necessary changes. Taking time to reflect on what's most important and making any necessary changes like setting new career goals, pursuing different hobbies, or spending more time with loved ones can help to prevent burnout from reoccurring.

Identify any potential triggers for burnout, such as overworking or taking on too many tasks at once, and take steps to avoid them. It's also important to communicate with your supervisor about your recovery plan and any accommodations you may want. This can include adjustments to your workload, schedule, or responsibilities, as well as support from colleagues or access to mental health resources. Be open and honest with your supervisor about your needs and limitations, and work together to develop a plan that works for both of you. Remember to take things one step at a time, and prioritize your well-being as you make your way back to work.

Sometimes, the symptoms of burnout can be too overwhelming to handle on your own. If you are experiencing severe symptoms or feel like you are not making any progress with your recovery plan, seeking professional help is a good idea. A mental health professional can help you identify the root causes of your burnout, develop coping strategies, and provide support as you work towards recovery.

There are several types of therapy that can be helpful for burnout, including cognitive-behavioral therapy (CBT), which helps individuals identify and challenge negative thought patterns, and mindfulness-based therapy, which focuses on developing present-moment awareness and reducing stress. A therapist can also help you identify any underlying mental health issues that may be contributing to your burnout and develop a treatment plan that addresses those issues.

Self-care is an important part of recovering from burnout. It involves taking care of yourself physically, emotionally, and mentally to reduce stress and improve overall well-being. Here are some self-care strategies that can help you recover from burnout:

Exercise regularly: Exercise has been shown to reduce stress and improve mood. Aim for at least 30 minutes of moderate-intensity exercise most days of the week.

Eat a healthy diet: Eating a diet rich in fruits, vegetables, whole grains, and lean protein can help you feel better physically and mentally.

Get enough sleep: Getting enough sleep is essential for recovery from burnout. Aim for 7-9 hours of sleep each night.

Practice relaxation techniques: Relaxation techniques like deep breathing, progressive muscle relaxation, and meditation can help reduce stress and improve mood.

Do things you enjoy: Engaging in hobbies and activities that you enjoy can help you relax and feel better emotionally.

Remember that burnout is a sign that something needs to change, and taking steps to address the root causes can help you feel better both at work and in your personal life.

A year ago, I made the decision to quit drinking. At the time, I didn't consider myself a heavy drinker, but looking back, I realize that my alcohol consumption had increased over the years without me even noticing. I had been using alcohol as a coping mechanism to deal with the demands of working in Corporate America, and it had become a habit that was difficult to break.

At the same time, I was experiencing burnout from my job. The long hours, high pressure, and constant demands had taken a toll on my mental and physical health. I was exhausted all the time, irritable, and felt like I was always on edge. I knew something had to change, but I wasn't sure what to do.

After some reflection, I realized that my drinking was contributing to my burnout. It was a way for me to numb my feelings of stress and overwhelm, but it was also making me feel worse in the long run. I decided to quit drinking, not just as a way to improve my physical health, but also my mental and emotional well-being.

The first few weeks were difficult. I had to find new ways to cope with stress and anxiety, and I missed the social aspect of drinking with friends and colleagues. But as time went on, I started to notice the positive changes. I had more energy, felt less irritable, and was better able to manage my stress, and quality of my sleep improved a lot. I was able to focus more on my work and felt more productive than ever before.

Quitting drinking also gave me the clarity to recognize what was causing my burnout and take steps to address it. I started setting boundaries at work, saying no to tasks that were not essential, and taking breaks throughout the day to recharge. I also started practicing mindfulness meditation and other relaxation techniques to manage my stress.

Looking back, quitting drinking was one of the best decisions I've ever made. It helped me recover from burnout and improve my overall well-being. I now have more clarity and focus in my work and personal life, and I'm grateful for the positive impact it has had on my mental and physical health.

The sober curious movement has helped many individuals like myself explore the benefits of sobriety and prioritize their health and well-being. Quitting drinking is no longer a stigma associated only with alcoholics; it's a personal decision that anyone can make to improve their quality of life.

Chapter 6: Creating a Sustainable Work-Life Balance

In today's fast-paced world, achieving a healthy work-life balance can seem like a daunting task. With work demands, family obligations, and personal goals, it can be difficult to find time for everything. However, creating a sustainable work-life balance is essential for both personal and professional success. In this chapter, we will explore the importance of creating a healthy work-life balance, techniques for managing time effectively and staying organized, and strategies for setting goals and managing expectations.

Maintaining a healthy work-life balance is crucial for our physical and mental health. When we work too much and neglect our personal lives, we risk burnout, stress, and other health problems. On the other hand, neglecting our work can lead to financial insecurity and career stagnation. Thus, achieving a healthy work-life balance is essential for our well-being and success.

In addition to the health benefits, a healthy work-life balance can also improve our productivity and creativity. When we take time to relax and recharge, we return to work with renewed energy and fresh perspectives. This can lead to better decision-making, problem-solving, and innovation.

Maintaining a healthy work-life balance is crucial for overall well-being. To achieve this, prioritizing tasks is essential. Start by identifying the most important tasks that need to be completed each day. By doing so, you can stay focused and avoid wasting time on low-priority activities.

In addition to prioritizing tasks, setting realistic goals is also important. Setting achievable goals for each day, week, or month can help you stay motivated and avoid feeling overwhelmed. Breaking tasks into smaller, more manageable pieces can also help you stay focused and avoid feeling overwhelmed.

In addition to the previous strategies mentioned for creating a sustainable work-life balance, it's also important to use a comprehensive calendar or planner. Keeping track of all work and personal tasks, no matter how small, in the same calendar can help you maintain a clear overview of your commitments and avoid double-booking or missing important events.

Include exact times and addresses of events in your calendar to help you plan your day more efficiently. Knowing when and where you need to be at a specific time can help you avoid last-minute stress and rush. Additionally, including important details such as what to bring or wear to an event can help you avoid scrambling to figure out what you need at the last minute.

When it comes to delegating tasks, it's important to not only free up time for more important activities but also to help develop the skills of others and build a stronger team. By delegating tasks to others, you can not only focus on the tasks that require your specific skillset and expertise but also help others grow in their role and contribute to the success of the team.

Limiting distractions is crucial to maintain a healthy work-life balance. Avoid distractions such as social media, email, or unnecessary meetings. This can help you stay focused and avoid wasting time on non-essential activities. Taking breaks throughout the day can help you stay refreshed and avoid burnout. Consider taking short breaks to stretch, go for a walk, or meditate.

When it comes to setting goals and managing expectations, being realistic is key. Set goals that are achievable within the time and resources available to you. Unrealistic goals can lead to frustration and burnout. Communicating your expectations clearly to others, including colleagues, managers, and family members, can help avoid misunderstandings and manage expectations.

Knowing your limits is important. Saying no to tasks or commitments that are beyond your capacity can help you avoid feeling overwhelmed and maintain a healthy work-life balance. Regularly evaluating your progress towards your goals and adjusting your plans as necessary can help you stay on track and avoid wasting time on activities that are not contributing to your goals.

In conclusion, creating a sustainable work-life balance requires prioritizing tasks, setting realistic goals, using a planner or calendar, delegating tasks, limiting distractions, taking breaks, being realistic, breaking tasks into smaller pieces, communicating expectations, saying no when necessary, and evaluating progress regularly. By following these strategies, you can achieve a healthy work-life balance and improve your overall well-being.

The fear of losing one's job can be a significant source of stress and anxiety, especially if you have debt and no emergency funds to fall back on. The constant worry of being fired can lead to burnout, which can negatively impact your overall well-being and job performance.

If you're experiencing financial stress, it's important to address your personal financial matters in addition to your work-life balance. Taking steps to manage your finances and build a financial safety net can help reduce your stress and anxiety levels and increase your overall sense of security.

One way to address your financial stress is to create a budget and stick to it. By tracking your income and expenses, you can gain a clearer understanding of where your money is going and identify areas where you can cut back. This can help you prioritize your spending and reduce your debt over time.

Building an emergency fund is also an important step towards financial security. By setting aside money in a savings account, you can create a safety net for unexpected expenses or income disruptions, such as losing your job.

Additionally, it's important to address any issues with your job performance or productivity that may be contributing to your fear of losing your job. Seeking feedback from your manager or colleagues and taking steps to improve your skills and knowledge can help you feel more confident and secure in your role.

By addressing your personal financial matters and taking steps to reduce your stress and anxiety levels, you can improve your overall sense of security and job performance.

Chapter 7: Cultivating Resilience

In high-stress jobs, resilience is crucial for maintaining a healthy work-life balance and preventing burnout. Resilience is the ability to adapt to and bounce back from setbacks, challenges, and adversity. Here are some techniques for building resilience:

Develop a growth mindset: A growth mindset is the belief that skills and abilities can be developed through hard work, dedication, and perseverance. Cultivating a growth mindset can help you view setbacks as opportunities for learning and growth. Developing a growth mindset has been a game-changer for me in my personal and professional life. As someone who used to have a fixed mindset, I would often become discouraged and give up when faced with challenges or setbacks. However, as I learned more about the concept of a growth mindset, I began to shift my perspective and approach to difficulties.

One practical example of developing a growth mindset is reframing negative self-talk. Instead of saying "I'm just not good at this" or "I'll never be able to do it," I now say "I haven't figured it out yet, but I will keep trying." By changing my internal dialogue, I have been able to approach challenges with more positivity and a willingness to learn.

Another way to cultivate a growth mindset is to embrace failure as a learning opportunity. In the past, I would avoid taking risks for fear of failure. But now, I view failure as a natural part of the learning process. When I encounter failure, I ask myself, "What can I learn from this experience?" By reframing failure in this way, I have been able to bounce back from setbacks more quickly and with more resilience.

Overall, developing a growth mindset is a powerful tool for building resilience and bouncing back from setbacks. By viewing challenges as opportunities for growth, we can approach difficulties with a more positive and constructive attitude, ultimately leading to greater success in both our personal and professional lives.

Practicing self-care is an important aspect of building resilience. It involves taking care of your physical, mental, and emotional health to help you better cope with stress and adversity. One way to practice self-care is to make time for regular exercise. Whether it's going for a run, taking a yoga class, or lifting weights, exercise can help boost your mood, reduce stress levels, and improve your overall health. These practices provide me with a sense of control and helps me feel more empowered to take on whatever comes my way.

Building a strong support network is crucial for building resilience in corporate America because it helps individuals feel less isolated and more connected to others. This can be especially important in high-stress work environments, where employees may feel like they are constantly battling against deadlines, difficult coworkers, or other challenges.

Having a support network of friends, family, and colleagues can provide a sounding board for ideas, help with problem-solving, and offer emotional support during difficult times. For example, if an employee is dealing with a difficult project or coworker, they can turn to a supportive colleague for advice or a listening ear. This can help alleviate stress and feelings of overwhelm.

Cultivating relationships with others also helps to build trust and a sense of camaraderie within a workplace. It can create a positive work culture where employees feel supported and valued, which can increase job satisfaction and engagement.

One practical example of building a strong support network in the workplace is through regular team building activities or offsite retreats. These events allow employees to get to know each other outside of work and build stronger connections that can translate to the workplace. Another example is to find a mentor within the company who can provide guidance and support, especially for employees who may be new to the company or industry.

Personally, I have experienced the benefits of having a strong support network at work. When I was working on a particularly challenging project, I was able to turn to a colleague who had experience in the same field for advice and support. Her guidance and encouragement helped me to stay focused and motivated, and ultimately, we were able to complete the project successfully. Additionally, having a close friend at work who I could confide in and share my struggles with made the job feel less daunting and more manageable.

Staying optimistic can be challenging, especially during difficult times in Corporate America. However, maintaining a positive outlook can help you maintain your motivation and focus on your goals. Research has shown that optimism can lead to better outcomes in various areas of life, including work.

One way to stay optimistic is to focus on the positives in any situation. Even during difficult times, try to find something to be grateful for or something to learn from the experience. For example, if you receive negative feedback from your boss on a project, try to view it as an opportunity to improve your skills and knowledge.

Another way to stay optimistic is to surround yourself with positive people. Being around optimistic and supportive individuals can help you maintain a positive outlook on life and work. Seek out colleagues or friends who are positive and encouraging, and try to spend more time with them.

It's also important to practice positive self-talk. This means using positive language when you speak to yourself, especially during times of stress or adversity. Instead of saying things like "I can't do this" or "this is too difficult," try saying things like "I can handle this" or "I'm capable of overcoming this challenge."

Additionally, setting realistic and achievable goals can help you stay optimistic. When you achieve a goal, no matter how small, it can give you a sense of accomplishment and motivate you to continue working towards your larger goals.

In summary, staying optimistic is essential for building resilience in Corporate America. By focusing on the positives, surrounding yourself with positive people, practicing positive self-talk, and setting realistic goals, you can maintain a positive outlook on life and work, even during difficult times. In addition to building resilience, it's important to stay motivated and focused during difficult times.

Celebrating your successes, no matter how small they may be, is a powerful tool for boosting your motivation and maintaining your focus. Recognizing your achievements and progress towards your goals can help you stay on track and build momentum towards further success. This can be particularly helpful when recovering from burnout, as it can be easy to get bogged down in feelings of overwhelm or failure.

One effective way to celebrate successes is to take time to reflect on what you have accomplished. This could involve journaling about your progress, sharing your achievements with a trusted friend or family member, or simply taking a moment to acknowledge your accomplishments and give yourself a pat on the back. It's important to remember that every step forward, no matter how small, is a step in the right direction.

Another way to celebrate your successes is to reward yourself for your hard work. This could be as simple as treating yourself to a favorite snack or indulging in a relaxing activity, such as a massage or a movie night. Setting up a reward system can be a fun and effective way to keep yourself motivated and engaged in your recovery process.

Finally, celebrating your successes can also involve sharing your journey with others. Whether you're part of a support group, a recovery program, or the sober curious movement, sharing your successes with others can help you feel connected, supported, and empowered. It can also inspire others who may be struggling with similar challenges.

Remember, celebrating your successes is not about being perfect or achieving everything all at once. It's about recognizing your progress, staying motivated, and building momentum towards your goals. So take the time to celebrate your achievements, no matter how small, and use them as fuel to keep moving forward on your journey towards recovery.

Staying flexible is an essential aspect of recovering from burnout. It's important to remember that setbacks and unexpected challenges can happen, and being able to adapt and adjust your plans accordingly can make all the difference in your recovery journey. Being flexible means staying open to new ideas and approaches, even if they may be different from what you initially planned. It can also mean being willing to change course if something isn't working.

One way to stay flexible is to keep an open mind and be receptive to feedback from others. Seeking out feedback from colleagues, friends, or a therapist can provide valuable insights into how you can improve your approach and better manage your stress. It's important to remember that feedback is not a criticism, but an opportunity for growth.

Additionally, staying flexible can mean reevaluating your goals and priorities as you progress through your recovery. As you gain new insights and perspectives, you may find that what was once important to you may no longer be as meaningful or necessary. Being open to adjusting your goals and priorities can help you stay aligned with what truly matters to you and prevent burnout from occurring again in the future.

Finally, staying flexible also means being kind to yourself and allowing for some level of imperfection. It's normal to experience setbacks or have days where you don't feel as productive or focused as you'd like. Rather than beating yourself up, try to approach these moments with compassion and curiosity. Ask yourself what you can learn from the experience and how you can use it as an opportunity for growth and improvement. Remember that recovery from burnout is a journey, and staying flexible and adaptable can help you navigate the ups and downs along the way.

In conclusion, building resilience and staying motivated and focused during difficult times is essential for maintaining a healthy work-life balance and preventing burnout. Practice self-care, cultivate a strong support network, stay optimistic, and set goals and create a plan to achieve them. Stay flexible and celebrate your successes, no matter how small, to maintain your motivation and focus.

Chapter 8: Finding Joy and Purpose in Your Work

For many of us, work takes up a significant portion of our time and energy. It can be easy to feel stuck in a routine, drained, or unfulfilled in our jobs. However, finding joy and purpose in your work is essential for your overall well-being and performance. It can also be helpful to remember why you chose this career in the first place. Take some time to reflect on what made you happy and fulfilled in your earlier years and how you can get that feeling back. In this chapter, we will explore ways to discover fulfillment and meaning in your career.

Identifying your core values and purpose is a crucial step in finding joy and purpose in your work, whether you work in Corporate America or any other field. By taking the time to reflect on what is most important to you in life and what motivates you, you can gain a better understanding of how your work can align with your values and purpose.

For example, if you are someone who is passionate about social justice, you may find fulfillment in a career that allows you to work towards creating positive social change. On the other hand, if personal growth is a core value for you, you may find joy in a career that offers opportunities for learning and development.

Once you have identified your core values and purpose, it's important to find ways to align your work with these values. This could involve seeking out projects or tasks that are in line with your values, or finding ways to incorporate your values into your daily work routine.

In Corporate America, finding joy and purpose in your work can be challenging, especially in a highly competitive and fast-paced environment. However, by focusing on your core values and purpose, you can create a sense of meaning and fulfillment in your work, which can lead to greater job satisfaction and better overall well-being.

Additionally, it's important to seek out opportunities for growth and development in your career, whether that's through training programs, mentorship, or seeking out new challenges. By continuously learning and growing in your career, you can stay engaged and motivated, and find greater joy and purpose in your work.

Next, reflect on your purpose or mission in life. What do you want to accomplish in your career and how does it align with your personal values? When you have a clear understanding of your core values and purpose, you can better align your work with what matters most to you.

Remember why you chose your career path in the first place. What made you excited about your work in the early days? Sometimes, we can lose sight of our passion and enthusiasm for our jobs as we get bogged down in routine and stress.

Think back to when you first started working in your field. What did you enjoy most? What parts of your job bring you the most satisfaction? Try to reconnect with those aspects. If you find meaning in helping others, consider mentoring a colleague or volunteering for a cause related to your field. If you enjoy solving complex problems, seek out new challenges or take on a project outside of your usual responsibilities. If you value creativity and innovation, look for opportunities to bring new ideas to your team.

It's also important to align your work with your core values and purpose. If your current job doesn't align with what you truly believe in, it can be difficult to find fulfillment. Consider whether your current company and role align with your personal values and what changes you can make to better align your work with your purpose.

It's true that work doesn't always have to be a passion in order to find meaning and purpose in it. Many people find fulfillment in simply doing a good job and contributing to their company's success. Even in the seemingly mundane world of Corporate America, there are opportunities to make a positive impact.

One way to find purpose in your work is to focus on the impact your company is making on the world. Many successful corporations have made a commitment to social corporate governance and are taking steps to reduce their environmental footprint or contribute to their communities. By aligning your values with your company's mission, you can find fulfillment in knowing that you are working towards a greater good.

Another way to find meaning in a Corporate America job is to use your free time to engage in charitable or community work. Many companies offer volunteer opportunities or support employee-led initiatives. By using your skills and resources to help others, you can find purpose and fulfillment beyond the walls of your office.

Ultimately, the key to finding joy and purpose in your work is to align it with your values and goals. Whether you find passion in the work itself or in the impact it has on the world, it's important to stay true to yourself and what motivates you. By doing so, you can find meaning and fulfillment in even the most mundane tasks.

Having a positive mindset can help you find joy and purpose in your work. Instead of focusing on the negative aspects of your job, try to reframe your thoughts to see the positive. Find ways to appreciate the challenges and opportunities that come with your job. Focus on what you can learn and how you can grow.

Practice gratitude by reflecting on what you are thankful for in your job. Celebrate your successes and the achievements of your colleagues. By cultivating a positive mindset, you can improve your well-being and performance at work.

Expanding your skillset can be a powerful way to find joy and purpose in your work. For example, if you work in finance, you may consider enrolling in a course to learn about sustainable investing, which can align with your values and help you feel more fulfilled in your work. Or, if you work in marketing, you could take on a new project that involves developing skills in social media advertising or graphic design.

Learning new skills can also boost your confidence in your job. For instance, if you're struggling to master a new software program, taking a course or attending a workshop can help you gain the skills you need to be more efficient and effective in your work. Additionally, acquiring new skills can help you stand out in your job and position you for promotions or new job opportunities.

Expanding your skillset can also allow you to explore new career paths or industries. For example, if you work in the medical field, you might take a course in healthcare administration to explore opportunities in management. Or, if you work in the technology industry, you could enroll in a course on artificial intelligence or machine learning to explore new possibilities in the field.

Overall, developing new skills can help you find joy and purpose in your work by allowing you to grow, learn, and advance in your career. So, look for opportunities to expand your knowledge and experience, and be open to new challenges and possibilities.

One way to find joy and purpose in your work is to build positive relationships with colleagues, clients, or customers. This can involve seeking out opportunities to collaborate with others on projects or initiatives, as well as building a supportive community within your workplace.

By working closely with others, you can gain new perspectives on your work and learn from their experiences. This can help you grow both personally and professionally, as well as make your work more enjoyable and fulfilling.

In addition to collaborating with colleagues, it's important to also build positive relationships with clients or customers. By providing exceptional service and building strong connections with those you serve, you can develop a sense of purpose and meaning in your work.

Building positive relationships in the workplace can also help to reduce stress and improve overall well-being. When you feel supported and connected to others in your workplace, you are more likely to feel satisfied and fulfilled in your job.

To build positive relationships, it's important to be open and approachable, and to actively listen to others. Seek out opportunities to connect with others, such as attending networking events or social gatherings, and take the time to get to know your colleagues on a personal level.

In addition, it's important to practice empathy and understanding in your interactions with others. By putting yourself in someone else's shoes and considering their perspective, you can build stronger relationships and create a more positive work environment.

Overall, building positive relationships in the workplace can have a significant impact on your well-being and sense of purpose in your work. By seeking out opportunities to collaborate and connect with others, you can create a supportive community and find greater fulfillment in your job.

In addition to finding joy and purpose in your work, it's important to also find meaning outside of your job. Pursuing hobbies and interests outside of work can help you cultivate a well-rounded life and achieve greater fulfillment overall. Whether it's playing a sport, painting, gardening, or cooking, find something that brings you joy and invest time and energy into it.

Connecting with family and friends is also crucial for finding meaning outside of work. Spend quality time with loved ones, whether it's having dinner together, going on a weekend trip, or simply chatting on the phone. These connections can provide a sense of support and belonging that can be deeply fulfilling.

Remember that when you have a fulfilling life outside of work, it can also benefit your work life. Engaging in activities and relationships that bring you joy and fulfillment can give you the energy and motivation to approach your work with greater enthusiasm and creativity. It can also provide you with the perspective and balance needed to navigate the challenges and stressors of the workplace.

Conclusion

Burnout is a serious problem in today's fast-paced work environment. It can affect anyone, regardless of their occupation or experience level. In this book, we've discussed the causes and symptoms of burnout, as well as strategies for preventing and recovering from it.

One of the most important things you can do to prevent burnout is to prioritize self-care. This means taking care of your physical, emotional, and mental health. Make sure you're getting enough sleep, exercise, and healthy food. Set boundaries around your work and make time for activities that bring you joy and relaxation.

If you're already experiencing burnout, it's important to take action to recover. This might mean taking time off work, seeking professional help, or implementing new strategies for managing your workload and stress levels.

Remember that finding joy and purpose in your work is also essential for preventing and recovering from burnout. This means aligning your work with your core values and purpose, developing new skills, building positive relationships with colleagues, and finding meaning outside of work.

By implementing these strategies, you can create a sustainable work-life balance and prevent burnout from taking over your life. It's important to remember that burnout is not a sign of weakness, but rather a natural response to an unhealthy work environment. By taking action and prioritizing your well-being, you can overcome burnout and thrive in your career.

Thank you for reading, and stay motivated!

www.ingramcontent.com/pod-product-compliance
Lightning Source LLC
Chambersburg PA
CBHW070801220526
45467CB00017B/705